EPHESIANS

How Jesus Creates a New People in a New World

An Everyday Discipleship Study

By Brad Watson

SATURATE PUBLISHING

EPHESIANS: How Jesus Creates a New People in a New World

Published by **Saturate**
1100 Bellevue Way NE
Suite 8A, #224
Bellevue, WA 98004
www.saturatetheworld.com

Unless otherwise noted, all Scripture quotations are taken from the English Standard Version®, Copyright © 2017 by Crossway Publishing.

ISBN:
Paperback: 978-1-7324913-4-2
eBook: 978-1-7324913-5-9

Cover and Book Design | Nathan Parry

Editing | Lisa Kukkamaa-Baker

Book Layout | Jeff M. Miller, FiveJsDesign.com

First Printing 2019

–PAUL, EPHESIANS 4:1–6

"I therefore, a prisoner for the Lord, urge you to walk in a manner worthy of the calling to which you have been called, with all humility and gentleness, with patience, bearing with one another in love, eager to maintain the unity of the Spirit in the bond of peace. There is one body and one Spirit—just as you were called to the one hope that belongs to your call—one Lord, one faith, one baptism, one God and Father of all, who is over all and through all and in all."

TABLE OF CONTENTS

INTRODUCTION TO SERIES

Each fall as a church in Los Angeles, we take eight to twelve weeks to teach through our core convictions, beliefs, and practices as a church. We often do this through sermons that outline the purpose and power of the gospel, our gospel identity, and the rhythms of life that overflow from the gospel.[1] It's more than a sermon series for us. These are the gospel basics, the primer, and the foundation on which everything we do as a missional church is laid.

You can read through these convictions on our website (*saturatetheworld.com*), or in Jeff Vanderstelt's book, *Saturate*, or you could even attend a Saturate training event or Soma School to have a deep dive instruction on them. We don't just train on these things as topics, they saturate every aspect of life in our church. They come out in each sermon, we sing them in our gatherings, and we find them through the whole of the Bible in both its grand narrative and in each particular scene or book of Scripture. It could honestly and humbly be said that this is our church's culture and the vision for the intentional and steady study of the Scriptures in our missional communities. This series of guided Bible studies is built around and from church cultures like ours from the ever-multiplying family of churches called Soma.

Our aim of this series is to help communities small and large engage the Scriptures from the context of the Story of God and grow deeper in the richness of understanding, speaking, and living the gospel of Jesus. Five core principles hold each of these studies together:

[1] If you're unfamiliar with these concepts, further explanation is given in the glossary of this study.

Discipleship Environment

Disciples are made in community on mission, and a disciple is someone who is increasingly submitting every aspect of life to God the Father, Son, and Spirit.

Holistic

Good theology isn't just understanding the truths of God in our heads, it is believing and applying the truths to our hearts, and it's obeying the truths in our everyday lives. A fully formed disciple is growing in their head, heart, and hands.

Bible

The Bible is the authoritative grand narrative of God's mission to restore all things. This is the true story of the entire world.

The Gospel

The good news of Jesus is He has defeated sin, death, and evil through His life, death, and resurrection and is making all things new, even us.

Empowered

Prayer is the oxygen of every gospel-focused community of disciples.

We believe that through each study, a community will be reintroduced to the foundations of discipleship while also growing in a deeper understanding of how the gospel applies to every aspect of life.

USING THIS GUIDE

This guide has been designed for disciples who are committed to the process of learning to find Jesus in such a way they see their lives and neighborhoods made new. Disciple-making environments create space for followers of Jesus to thrive by repeated reintroduction of the gospel to the hearts of each disciple. This guide is designed to facilitate that type of space.

This guide can work well in multiple settings. It can be used on your own as a personal and enriching study. Large community groups, like a weekly meal within a missional community, can adapt it for their purposes. Or smaller groups, like what many Soma churches call DNA Groups when two or three disciples meet together, can use it to facilitate study and connection. You are an expert in the communities and disciples you're leading. Use it in whatever context you believe is most beneficial.

Personal Reading and Reflection: The Four Questions

In preparation for each week, we encourage each participant to take time to read the passage and reflect on how it introduces us to the gospel. Use these four questions that help disciples focus their Scripture reading on the gospel of God.

1. **Who is God?**—What does this passage tell us about God's character, motives, and identity? The Bible is about Him.
2. **What Has He Done?**—What do we see God doing in this passage? What work do we observe?
3. **Who Are We?**—What does this passage tell us about our identity?
4. **How Do We Live?**—Lastly, how is God calling us to live based on who we are, what He has done, and who He is?

This is important because personal reading and reflection are a crucial part of a disciple's journey and they allow each person the opportunity to come into the group discussions ready to engage.

Holistic Discussions: Head, Heart, and Hands

Each week has a short opening article to set the table for your time, followed by a reading of the passage and discussion about what the passage means. Then, you move to applying the truths of the Bible to your own heart before thinking through what obedience to that passage will look like. This is a holistic study of an entire person. We call these different pieces Head, Heart, and Hands.

Head

Our minds are renewed by the knowledge of God, allowing Him to change what and how we think.

Heart

Our souls are restored by the application of truth to our wounds, stories, suffering, and sin.

Hands

Our everyday lives are transformed through the power of the Spirit to call us into obedience to the truth.

Extras

We've included "Extras" in each section that will provide insights into the text. This is intended to be supplemental and give extra linguistic, cultural, or modern context to the Scriptures.

Prayer

Each week we will guide you to pray. We're not going to throw a ton of instructions your way about that. But we urge you to pause and pray. Respond to God, talk to God, and listen to God in community.

Make It Your Own

Lastly, there's freedom! If you're leading a group, we suggest reading through this guide on your own in its entirety and then mapping out how your group will engage this tool. For example, you may decide your group would benefit from each person doing each week on their own before getting together to walk through each person's "highlights" or key questions you want to discuss as a group. Or you may decide your group would most benefit from walking through the entire thing together. Or you may decide on a mixture of those two approaches. Either way, know you have complete freedom.

INTRODUCTION TO EPHESIANS

Have you ever watched the "Director's Commentary" on your favorite movie? If you're a nerd like me, I'm sure you have. In the commentary, you get to watch the entire movie, but instead of listening to the original soundtrack and dialogue, you get to listen to the director and usually the screenwriter talk about each scene. They dive into the plot, lighting, important bits of dialogue, nuances, and back stories. Essentially, you're welcomed into the depths of the story and discover insights into what exactly is happening, what the writer's intent really was, and it adds a whole new level of understanding. If you know the story, these "movie extras" are incredible! However, if you've never seen the film and don't know the story, the director's commentary is simply noise.

Ephesians functions like the Director's Commentary to the Story of God. It's written to the Church to remind us of the Story, to tell us once again: "This is what was going on when Jesus died and rose again." Paul is pulling back the curtain and saying, "You might not have noticed, but when you were saved, you were saved into a Church, and the Church was created for God's purposes. Maybe you weren't fully aware, but this New Life is ushered in and upheld by both the power and grace of God."

Paul is giving us the "movie extras" to the greatest story ever told. It's the true story of the cosmos, humanity, and God's relentless pursuit to make Himself known. Here's the SparkNotes version of that Story:

Creation

In the beginning, God created everything and it was good. He created humans to reflect His glory and goodness. To be united to Him and with one another. The world was thriving and bustling with joy, purpose, and even understanding.

Promise

But God promised to defeat sin, evil, and death and make the world new. He chose Abraham to be the father of a family that would bless all the peoples of the world. Through their uniqueness, obedience, and worship, the world would once again see what God is like. But most pressing, God promised that through His family, a King would come who would redeem the world from sin, death, and evil.

Restoration

One day, Jesus will return, rule, and restore all creation. All sin, death, and suffering from evil will be wiped away. God will dwell with His people and we will worship Him forever, just as we were created to: delighting in God's loving resolve to restore us and His world.

Rebellion

Later, humanity rebelled against the living God who created them, knew them, and provided abundant life for them. Sinning against God, they seemingly broke the world forever. Shame, guilt, destruction, murder, pride, greed, and many more sins rushed into the world. All human life orbited around sin, death, and evil.

Redemption

Jesus is that King. The good news about Jesus is that through His life, death, and resurrection He has defeated sin, death, and evil and is making all things new, including humanity!

Church

Jesus sends His Spirit into all who believe, and they're called not just into salvation but into the people of God—the Church. The Church is a remarkable resurrected family that exists in this world as a signpost of the gospel and agents of reconciliation in a world still gripped with death.

These symbols were created by Kevin Platt and Chris Gonzalez and used with permission.

That is the story Paul expects to be in his readers' minds as he describes the power of the gospel, the Church, and our mission in this world.

Ephesians is all about how the Father, Son, and Spirit have created a whole new people and a whole new world. Paul describes the overwhelming power of God to make all things new, including our lives, including our neighbors, and including our planet.

What's going on in your life, Ephesians tells us, is more incredible than you know. What's going on in our world is more beautiful than we imagine. Who we are as the Church is far more sacred and purposeful than we ever dreamed!

In this letter, who the Church is, what the Church is, and how the Church lives takes center stage. This is our moment of the story. This is who we are.

THE STORY OF
THE CHURCH IN EPHESUS AND PAUL

The church of Ephesus is an incredible testament to the global Church and God's masterful plan to start churches.

The story of Ephesus actually begins in a bustling city in the Middle East called Antioch. It was an amazing city at the cross sections of the entire known world. It connected Asia, Africa, and Europe. It was also the first place where disciples of Jesus were called Christians (Acts 11). The Church began as disciples fled persecution in Jerusalem. As they settled in Antioch, they not only proclaimed the good news about Jesus to Jews but also to Greeks, and one of the most influential churches of the first century was born.

This incredibly diverse church grew rapidly as Barnabas moved from Jerusalem to help lead it. He developed and equipped a fantastic group of leaders too. In fact, one of the people he recruited to join him was Saul of Tarsus, or known mostly to us as Paul, the author of Ephesians. Barnabas and Paul co-led this urban church together, forming a strong leadership team and equipping an incredible number of Jews, Greeks, and Africans in the gospel and way of Jesus.

Barnabas was known as a wonderful trainer and encourager in the gospel. Paul was known mostly as being a persecutor of Christians who had been converted radically on the road to Damascus. He was raised among the religious and academic elites. He knew the Jewish law, kept the law, and persuaded others to follow the law. Often, that persuasion was combative. However, in coming to Christ, he came to see not just the truth of the gospel of Jesus but the awesome beauty and power of the grace of God made clear and tangible through Jesus.

The church in Antioch was always looking outside its own city. It cared for the financial and physical needs of other churches in other regions too. So, it wasn't surprising that as this church grew in influence in its own city that it was also called by the Holy Spirit to send others out to start new churches across the world. The elders, in a moment of fasting, worship, and prayer, knew that God was sending Barnabas and Paul out of Antioch toward Europe. They started by planting churches across Turkey before returning to Antioch to give reports. Paul then embarked on a second round, this time going through Turkey into Greece, taking with him a growing team of men and women.

Paul first came to Ephesus, a coastal city in Greece, on a very short stint, with a couple, Priscilla and Aquila. They went to the synagogue there and reasoned with the Jews about the resurrection and the gospel. Paul went back to Jerusalem and Antioch, but Priscilla and Aquila stayed to continue sharing the gospel with the Jews and Greeks. Then came a teacher, Apollos, from the North African city of Alexandria, which had also become a massive central hub for the gospel. He came debating persuasively and teaching about Jesus. With the help of Priscilla and Aquila, he grew in his understanding of the depths of the gospel and continued teaching before moving to another city.

Paul came back to Ephesus, this time for three years. This became one of the longest stays of Paul's life. He saw the church birthed and watched it grow. Here Paul performed incredible miracles, preached the kingdom of God, not just in the synagogue but for years in a lecture hall in the center of the city. In those halls, thousands upon thousands of people heard the gospel explained. The city was a "doorway" to the world, a merchant city, and by making this Paul's headquarters, people throughout the region were exposed to the gospel as they traveled through. Through Paul's teaching, they equipped teams that were sent all over the area, starting new churches, including in Laodicea and Colossi.

The church of Ephesus grew rapidly. However, as the church grew and people came to believe the gospel and walked away from the idols of the city, those in power became distressed. At a crucial juncture, Paul exorcised a demon very publicly, so that many believed in Jesus and walked away from their false religions and practices of magic, further worrying those in authority. The city was changing!

As more people abandoned the worship of the gods of the city, those who created the idols and those who made money from their worship and the industries surrounding it became angry. It resulted in a massive riot as the powers of the world and the powers of darkness were confronted with the power of the gospel in their city. But after the unrest died down, Paul left Ephesus once more and for the last time.

During Paul's years in Ephesus he shared life, he shared meals, he shared moments of sorrow and joy. He was not just an evangelist in Ephesus; he was a shepherd to a community of saints. On his final journey, which was destined to end in years of imprisonment in Jerusalem then Rome, he met with the leaders of the church of Ephesus in a nearby town. There they wept, and Paul gave this farewell address:

You know that from day one of my arrival in Asia, I was with you totally—laying my life on the line, serving the Master no matter what, putting up with no end of scheming by Jews who wanted to do me in. I didn't skimp or trim in any way. Every truth and encouragement that could have made a difference to you, you got. I taught you out in public and I taught you in your homes, urging Jews and Greeks alike to a radical life-change before God and an equally radical trust in our Master Jesus.

But there is another urgency before me now. I feel compelled to go to Jerusalem. I'm completely in the dark about what will happen when I get there. I do know that it won't be any picnic, for the Holy Spirit has let me know repeatedly and clearly that there are hard times and imprisonment ahead. But that matters little. What matters most to me is to finish what God started: The job the Master Jesus gave me of letting everyone I meet know all about this incredibly extravagant generosity of God.

And so this is good-bye. You're not going to see me again, nor I you, you whom I have gone among for so long proclaiming the news of God's inaugurated kingdom. I've done my best for you, given you my all, held back nothing of God's will for you.

Now it's up to you. Be on your toes—both for yourselves and your congregation of sheep. The Holy Spirit has put you in charge of these people—God's people they are—to guard and protect them. God himself thought they were worth dying for.

I know that as soon as I'm gone, vicious wolves are going to show up and rip into this flock, men from your very own ranks twisting words so as to seduce disciples into following them instead of Jesus. So stay awake and keep up your guard. Remember those three years I kept at it with you, never letting up, pouring my heart out with you, one after another.

Now I'm turning you over to God, our marvelous God whose gracious Word can make you into what he wants you to be and give you everything you could possibly need in this community of holy friends.

I've never, as you so well know, had any taste for wealth or fashion. With these bare hands I took care of my own basic needs and those who worked with me. In everything I've done, I have demonstrated to you how necessary it is to work on behalf of the weak and not exploit them. You'll not likely go wrong here if you keep remembering that our Master said, 'You're far happier giving than getting.' (Acts 20:18-35, The Message)

Those were the words Paul shared. The next they heard from him was through his teammates, through leaders like Timothy, whom Paul sent to help strengthen the church, and through his own letter. That's the story of Ephesus and Paul. What we have in the book of Ephesians is the letter within that story.

In this letter, Paul is reminding them of everything essential to Christians and every church: The gospel changes everything. It changes who you are, it changes the world we live in, it changes how we live, and it changes why we live. Ephesians is the letter about the Church written to the Church.

Let's jump into this letter not only for that specific church, but for the universal Church—a letter inspired by the Holy Spirit for you, me, and every communion of saints the world will ever know.

WEEK 1

A CHURCH ADOPTED

WEEK 1

Ephesians 1:1-14

● PERSONAL REFLECTION: FOUR QUESTIONS

Spend time reading this passage and reflecting on these questions in order. Think through all the explicit and implied statements about who God is, then what He has done, who we are, and how we should live. As you answer these questions, you can even connect them to each other. For example: If that's what God has done, who does that make me? And how do I live in light of that truth?

- **Who is God?**

- **What has He done?**

- **Who are we?**

- **How do we live?**

INTRODUCTION

On seven peaceful acres in the hill country of Texas, my grandparents have an ever-extending table. They must have ten leaves they can add to make room for any guests. Chairs appear out of rooms, closets, and even their barn. I grew up around this table. Even as a child, I was welcomed to it. I sat on a chair with a stack of books and a belt buckled around my waist and the back of the chair to keep me from falling.

The only thing that outnumbered the people around the table was the food on top of it. I often wondered what kind of magical wood created this platform that could sustain the weight of both the comfort and food—and elbows. It didn't matter who you were, as you sat at that table, you were identified by the one seated at the head as he reached out his hands and gathered his herd. He prayed graciously and simply, then uttered the final words of the liturgy: "Grab root and growl." I know Greek, Hebrew, Portuguese, and English, and I still don't understand the words, but I understand what it means: "Eat."

As I grew older, I realized this table was the center of life—not just for my family, but for their community. The people gathered around were welcomed as family, but it wasn't biology that bound us. It was the invitation of my grandparents, their love, their preparation of fajitas, BBQ, and so many other specialties. I also realized this was their theology, missiology, and ecclesiology all wrapped into one. For decades, from Texas to Panama, and in English and Spanish, they welcomed teenagers, mothers, soldiers, doctors, elderly, siblings, coaches, and anyone else to the table—into the family.

The opening lines of Ephesians are a poem of worship about the glory and majesty of God the Father and His remarkable work in Jesus to adopt us into His family. We're welcomed not just to a feast, but into every spiritual blessing that could ever be offered a human soul—we're with God and the recipients of His love. We are given an eternal inheritance purchased on the cross, secured in the empty tomb, and sealed by the giving of the Holy Spirit that inhabits us. Through the gospel, as Paul writes in this letter, we are empty tombs now filled with the grace, love, and power of God. This is who we are.

Later in this letter, Paul describes this grace as a mystery for himself but also for every believer. And it is just that. It's a profound and beautiful mystery of God's incredible grace to bless us as His children with everything we could ever need in Christ.

READ EPHESIANS 1:1-14 OUT LOUD.

HEAD:

Discuss this passage together.

- *What do these verses tell us about God?*

- *What does this tell us about God's work?*

- *What does it tell us about ourselves?*

- *How would we say this same passage in our own words?*

THE POWER OF ADOPTION

J.I. Packer put it simply in *Knowing God*:

What is a Christian? The question can be answered in many ways, but the richest answer I know is that a Christian is one who has God for his Father...Adoption is the highest privilege that the gospel offers: higher even than justification. To be right with God the Judge is a great thing, but to be loved and cared for by God the Father is greater.

Our highest privilege and deepest need is to experience the holy God as our loving Father, to approach Him without fear, and to be assured of His fatherly care and concern.

When the Holy Spirit takes up residence in our lives, we too can cry, "Abba, Father." The same Spirit that proceeds from the relationship between the Father and Son is implanted in us. The difference between us and Jesus is that He is the natural Son of the Father, whereas we are adopted into the family through His sacrifice.

Apart from Jesus, we are all spiritual orphans. Our rebellious and sinful nature cut us off from God the Father. The Bible says quite clearly that we are not born children of God and therefore must go through an adoption process. The price of our adoption was the death of God's Son. C.S. Lewis wrote in *Mere Christianity*, "The Son of God became a man to enable men to become the sons of God."

HEART:

This passage describes our unconditional adoption into God's family to bring the Father glory and Jesus praise. We often abandon this truth in our hearts, or it feels distant. Use these questions to dig deeper.

- *Where in your life do you feel abandoned? Why?*

- *Where do you feel like you need to earn acceptance? Why?*

- *When do you desire glory and praise? Why?*

- *Thinking about your story and this passage, how has God glorified Himself by making you an heir?*

HANDS:

This passage also describes the Holy Spirit as the mark of our adoption. A Christian who lives a life empowered by the Spirit will be reminded of who Jesus is and what He taught, of His character, and their identity in Christ. The Spirit gives us power to speak the gospel and demonstrate the gospel, to be disciples and make disciples. Essentially, the Holy Spirit compels us to glorify God.

- *How can you make space in your life to listen to what the Holy Spirit tells you about Jesus, your identity, and God's glory?*

- *What would it look like to live as family with the Church?*

PRAY

Spend time praying for each other as you reflect on this passage and your own lives. Pray to be empowered by the Spirit as you walk in obedience.

WEEK 2

A Church Belonging to Jesus

WEEK 2

Ephesians 1:15-23

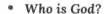

PERSONAL REFLECTION: FOUR QUESTIONS

Spend time reading this passage and reflecting on these questions in order. Think through all the explicit and implied statements about who God is, then what He has done, who we are, and how we should live. As you answer these questions, you can even connect them to each other. For example: If that's what God has done, who does that make me? And how do I live in light of that truth?

- **Who is God?**

- **What has He done?**

- **Who are we?**

- **How do we live?**

INTRODUCTION

If you've ever tried to get fit with a personal trainer or been on an athletic team or attended a motivational seminar, you've heard the appeal to consider your motivation and craft one. Envision your healthy body; let that drive you. Think about the trophy ceremony; it will fuel your practices. Consider your fortune, fame, and family; let that keep you working hard and pursuing your dreams.

Our motivations map our hopes. They tell us what we long for, what sustains us, and where we want to end up. But our motivations also tell us why. Why we live. Why we work. Why we hope. Something rarely examined is our motivation for the Church. Why are we part of the Church? What keeps us connected to it? What drives the Church? What sustains the Church? Why does the Church exist?

In Ephesians 1:15-23, Paul continues his exhortation and blessing to the people of the church in Ephesus. But now, he's talking about why he prays, how he prays for this church, and what motivates his entire life. Hint: it's Christ. The fact that Jesus was raised to life and seated at the right hand of God is his motivation for everything. Paul says, "Christ is the head over all things." Jesus has a Church, and the Church has power through Jesus. It's everything.

READ EPHESIANS 1:15-23 OUT LOUD.

HEAD:

Discuss this passage together. Warning: these are some of the most eloquent and powerfully structured sentences in the New Testament.

- **What do these verses tell us about God?**

- **What does this tell us about what God did and still does through Jesus?**

- **What does it tell us about the Church, the body?**

- **How would we put this passage in our own words?**

THE BODY OF CHRIST

This is one of those passages where you find the key Greek word, *soma*. This Greek word is used throughout the New Testament for "body," particularly used to describe the Church. *Soma* is used to describe two fundamental aspects of the Church:

1. The Church as the incarnation of Jesus. Meaning, the Church collective displays the good news of Jesus in our world.

2. The Church as an interconnected and interdependent community. Meaning, each person in the Church is connected to and dependent on the others. Likewise, each person contributes and is crucial to the thriving of the others.

Paul purposefully chose this word throughout his writings because it captures who we are as the Church: not just a group of people that meet once a week, but a present and unified family displaying the good news of Jesus in the places God has sent us throughout the world.

HEART:

This passage tells us Jesus is over all things. He has authority and is King over everything! If that's true, how does that change how we view our lives?

- **Where in your life do you feel out of control? Why?**

- **Where do you feel like you need to make a name for yourself? Why?**

- **When do you struggle with Jesus's authority in the Church? Why?**

- **Thinking about your story and this passage, how have you seen the power of resurrection in your life?**

HANDS:

Paul says that he writes and prays for the Church so they might "know the hope they have and the immeasurable greatness of His power toward us."

- *What would it look like to have this posture and motivation toward your missional community, household, and friends who don't believe?*

- *What would change in our neighborhood/city if it knew the hope of the gospel?*

- *How will our community take a step of obedience in what we've learned?*

PRAY

Spend time praying for each other as you reflect on this passage and your own lives. Pray to be empowered by the Spirit as you walk in obedience.

WEEK 3

A Church Raised by Grace

WEEK 3

Ephesians 2:1-10

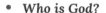

PERSONAL REFLECTION: FOUR QUESTIONS

Spend time reading this passage and reflecting on these questions in order. Think through all the explicit and implied statements about who God is, then what He has done, who we are, and how we should live. As you answer these questions, you can even connect them to each other. For example: If that's what God has done, who does that make me? And how do I live in light of that truth?

- **Who is God?**

- **What has He done?**

- **Who are we?**

- **How do we live?**

INTRODUCTION

Jesus began His ministry preaching, teaching, and healing. He loved the weak, the sick, and those destroyed by the world.

He became famous for who He ate with—tax collectors, prostitutes, the poor, the unclean. Then, sitting at a table, He hears His critics, "Who is this man that eats with such terrible people?" And He says, "It's not the healthy that need a doctor, but the sick," adding, "I came for sinners."

When Jesus says, "I came for the sick," I think, "Yes! I'm sick, heal me. Make me well! I've got lots of problems." When He says, "I came for the sinners," it's shocking. I understand my brokenness but bristle at the idea that I'm a sinner. We might respond to Jesus: "I thought you came for me. I'm not the problem; the disease is." However, Jesus says, "Come to the table; you're in need of grace."

Grace is my favorite doctrine I hardly believe. Functionally, I believe in merit alone for myself but grace alone for others. One, I don't think I need it. Two, I want to deserve it.

Here's the thing: merit-based privileges feel better. I want to walk into the kingdom standing tall, crowds cheering, and Jesus saying: "You deserve to be here all on your own." I'm happy to speak of the grace of God for others, but in my own heart, I wonder if I need it.

But the image of Jesus with friends, at tables, on boats, in courts, spread on a cross, and alive in the garden shakes me to my knees as I see His goodness and my own weakness. When I read Ephesians 2, I come to this conclusion: I need grace. The way of Jesus is the way. It's the way of the most love, the greatest hope, the best life. We cannot live our "best lives now" apart from God's grace.

In Ephesians 2:1-10, Paul describes grace. The human heart can hardly conceive of a world where grace is the highest truth. Where God's mercy triumphs over death. Where God's love outlasts our sin. But Paul says it does. And not only that, but Paul says in this passage that God's grace shown to us is immeasurable.

READ EPHESIANS 2:1-10 OUT LOUD.

HEAD:

Discuss this passage together.

- *How would we put this passage in our own words?*

- *What do these verses tell us about ourselves?*

- *Who are we apart from Christ, and who are we in Christ?*

- *Why has God done what He has done?*

- *What's the purpose of this grace?*

While this is a very evangelistic passage that outlines the gospel extraordinarily well, this letter was written to people very rooted in the faith. In fact, Ephesus was one of the most mature churches in the Ancient Roman Empire.

- **Why would Paul write these things to people who we would assume had already heard this before?**

GRACE IS HARD TO GRASP

Sometimes we need pictures and parables to understand grace. Consider watching this clip from *Les Miserables*, where Jean Valjean robs a church only to receive grace in return. (*http://bit.ly/GraspGrace*) It marks him for life. Having received the free gift of hospitality, an advocate, and mercy, he goes on to live a life of freedom—not merely from prison, but from possessions. He becomes a defender of the weak, a father to an orphan, and a person of great sacrifice. Also, consider watching all of *Les Misérables*; the whole thing is about our struggle with grace and law.

HEART:

This passage tells us we are dead in our trespasses and sins but alive because of God's mercy and love for us. This is often hard to swallow. We often believe we should get what we deserve, both the good and the bad. But the gospel of grace says we all deserve death but get life.

- *Where in your life do you feel you're getting what you deserve? Where do you want to earn it?*

- *How does the concept of earning love, affection, and mercy impact your relationship with God and others?*

- *How have you experienced God's grace in the past?*

HANDS:

In the conclusion of this passage, Paul says we are God's masterpiece created for good works that God prepared for us to walk in. The gospel has raised us from the dead and given us a new identity.

- *What would it look like to live your life knowing your identity is "masterpiece"?*

- *What is Jesus calling you to walk in?*

PRAY

Spend time praying for each other as you reflect on this passage and your own lives. Pray to be empowered by the Spirit as you walk in obedience.

WEEK 4

A Church without Borders

WEEK 4

Ephesians 2:11-22

PERSONAL REFLECTION: FOUR QUESTIONS

Spend time reading this passage and reflecting on these questions in order. Think through all the explicit and implied statements about who God is, then what He has done, who we are, and how we should live. As you answer these questions, you can even connect them to each other. For example: If that's what God has done, who does that make me? And how do I live in light of that truth?

- **Who is God?**

- **What has He done?**

- **Who are we?**

- **How do we live?**

INTRODUCTION

My family moved to Lisbon, Portugal two weeks after I turned eleven. Upon arrival, we had to go through a long process to become legal residents. We had just landed in a beautiful country we knew hardly anything about. People spoke a language we didn't know, and there was a rhythm of life with deep currents we weren't privy to. All this was an exciting adventure for an eleven-year-old until it came time to stand in line at the immigration office.

The line grew from the office downstairs and around the block. We were standing there with Eastern Europeans, Africans, and South Americans. I had spent my entire life feeling at home. This was the first time I didn't. Etched into my identity from that moment on was the label "Estrangeiro"–stranger, foreigner. It shaped many of my actions and thoughts as something I was ashamed of and wanted to compensate for, something that marked me as being apart, a forever outsider. Moving to Portugal changed me.

This is what life often feels like. We're on the outside, looking in. Maybe we get in, but we don't belong. Maybe we're here but strangers.

This happens within the life of the Church too. We can think, "I wasn't here when this church got started. I don't live in this part of town. I wasn't raised in the church. I come from a broken family. I don't see things the way everyone else does. I'm not gifted like everyone else. My finances don't match up. Sure, I can be part of the church, but I don't belong."

Paul says, no, you've been brought all the way to the center of the family and purpose of God. Welcome to the Church. Welcome home.

In Ephesians 2:11-22, Paul turns his attention toward the reality of the Church, these would-be-dead but now raised-to-life humans. Paul does this by telling the church they're a family, a household, a body, a people of promise, and the temple itself.

READ EPHESIANS 2:11-22 OUT LOUD.

HEAD:

Discuss this passage together.

- **What does this passage say about the Church?**

- **What are the metaphors Paul uses and what do they mean?**

- **What do these verses tell us about what Jesus has done in shaping the Church?**

- **Why do you think it's important to remember that we were once far off from God?**

- **What does it mean that we are now near and part of the covenant?**

- **How would you put this passage in your own words?**

COVENANT DEFINED

What is Paul referring to when he writes: "Remember... you were alienated from the commonwealth of Israel, and strangers to the covenants of promise, having no hope and without God in the world"? He's talking about the rich commitments and promises God made in revealing Himself to the people of Israel to bless the entire world. Here's a quick summary of the covenants God made.

- In Genesis 11, and multiple times afterward, God promises to make Abraham into a big and blessed family, and that through that family, God would bless the entire world.
- In Exodus 19, God promises to Moses and all the people rescued from bondage in Egypt that He would make them a nation, a kingdom of priests. They would be a holy people who would worship God and show the world what God is like.
- In 2 Samuel, God promises to David that from his line, God would bring a king who would rule and bring peace to Israel and the world.

All of these covenants build on each other, and they all meant something to each generation. They were marked, set-apart, God's holy and beloved people He was using to redeem and bless all humanity. Also, within those covenants, you can see that anyone who wasn't part of Abraham's family was an alien, a stranger, a foreigner to the power, presence, and purposes of God.

Paul calls us to remember we once were on the outside, looking in. We didn't have a hope at all for the brokenness of the world. We weren't part of the family of God. We were far off. Our view of the world was without the presence of God. We had no concept of the place of God, things of God, or love of God.

We want to go back into our stories, find the victims we made, and the victims we became. Which is good. However, Paul says remember not just the sin and death you were in, but who you were in relation to God. Your story was once a solo, a monologue. You lived in brokenness without hope. Remember the alienation, the isolation. But God has brought you into His ever-expanding family! This is grace, part two. Not only were you dead, you were also alienated. Not only were you raised to life, you were also brought into the center of God's family and mission.

HEART:

This passage says we needed Jesus to preach peace to those of us who were far off and those who were near. In fact, he says we were far from God, and now we've been brought near. The presence and dwelling of God within the Church is the grand reward. God's presence comes to us, because of the gospel, declaring: "There is no war between us any longer. I'm for you and with you."

- *How do you experience God's presence within the life of your missional community? Small group? Local church?*

- *How does this truth create unity within the body?*

HANDS:

At its heart, this passage is saying that the covenant partnership and people of God are now bringing all these people (us!) into the church because of Jesus. It also describes a church with a variety of citizens and members.

- *What would it look like to live your life knowing you are on the mission of God (redeeming and restoring the world)?*

- *What would it take to live your life as an integral part of the family of God?*

PRAY

Spend time praying for each other as you reflect on this passage and your own lives. Pray to be empowered by the Spirit as you walk in obedience.

WEEK 5

A CHURCH FOR GOD'S MISSION

WEEK 5

Ephesians 3:1-13

PERSONAL REFLECTION: FOUR QUESTIONS

Spend time reading this passage and reflecting on these questions in order. Think through all the explicit and implied statements about who God is, then what He has done, who we are, and how we should live. As you answer these questions, you can even connect them to each other. For example: If that's what God has done, who does that make me? And how do I live in light of that truth?

- **Who is God?**

- **What has He done?**

- **Who are we?**

- **How do we live?**

INTRODUCTION

The cul-de-sac was a phenomenal invention for the suburbs. It created a safe and peaceful place for families to raise children.

No one passed through. The only time strangers can appear is after making a wrong turn and finding themselves at a dead end. The design made it simple for those who don't belong to quickly turn around.

It also kept everyone who belonged there in one place. Once you came in, you didn't have to leave. You could remain the rest of your days with like-minded folks, playing games in your asphalt sanctuary.

The cul-de-sac is the epitome of the suburban life and values. However, the gospel is not a cul-de-sac. It isn't a safe sanctuary that separates you from the dangers of the world—it throws you into the world. It isn't your private enclave to secure your values and doctrines. It ushers you into a hospitality for the other, the not-like-you. The gospel is doctrinal, changing what we believe. It is also personal, changing who we are. But it is more than that. What God does in us, He intends to do through us.

Those who follow Jesus join His mission by making disciples of all ethnic groups by going, teaching, and baptizing (Matt. 28:18-20). We are sent to teach, speak, counsel, discuss, and proclaim the gospel to others so that they might be baptized into God's new creation and join His mission of making all things new. We are called "ambassadors of reconciliation" and given the privilege of sharing in Jesus's ministry of reconciling the world to Himself (2 Cor. 5:17-20). Those who have been changed by the gospel share its life-changing power with others. We should announce and embody the good news by caring for the poor and rebuilding cities (Is. 61:4). In fact, the future for the people of God is an entirely new city in a new creation (Rev. 21). The Church should be a movie trailer of this grand, coming attraction when all things will be made new!

Christopher Wright wrote well about this reality in *The Mission of God*:

> *Mission is not ours; mission is God's. Certainly, the mission of God is the prior reality out of which flows any mission that we get involved in. Or, as has been nicely put, it is not so much the case that God has a mission for His Church in the world but that God has a Church for His mission in the world. Mission was not made for the Church; the Church was made for mission—God's mission.*

In Ephesians 3:1-13, Paul wraps up the first half of his letter, which is all about the depths of the gospel. While chapter 2 highlighted the power of the gospel, chapter 3 talks about the purpose of the gospel: that what God has done in you (Ephesians 2), God wants to also do through you (Ephesians 3:1-13). The good news isn't just for us, it's for the world.

READ EPHESIANS 3:1-13 OUT LOUD.

HEAD:

Discuss this passage together.

- **What does this passage say about God and what He's done?**

- **What do these verses tell us about Paul, how he viewed himself and his work?**

- **What do these verses tell us about who we are as the Church and how we ought to live?**

- **How would you put this passage in your own words?**

NOT JUST FOR PAUL

When we come to Christ, we are all sent on His mission. We are new and have a new purpose. Christ reconciled us to Himself and we are a new creation. Our old way of finding identity and our broken ways of finding meaning are over. We are reconciled and ushered into a vibrant and living relationship with God. This is the gospel, that Christ has reconciled us to God through His death and resurrection and is making all things new—even us. We are recipients of the gospel, messengers of the gospel, and servants of the gospel. We cannot separate our identity in Christ from our purpose in Christ. Our renewed identity and purpose require some sort of expression of gospel-focused community on mission:

- We live on mission because we have received the gospel.
- We live on mission because we are messengers of the gospel. He is making His appeal to the world through us.
- We live on mission because we are ministers of reconciliation—servants of the gospel.
- We live on mission because we are ambassadors—representatives of the gospel.

We cannot separate our identity in Christ from our purpose in Christ.

HEART:

In this passage, Paul talks about the privilege and honor it is to make the mystery of the gospel known to people who are far off.

- *Does it feel the same for you? Can you relate?*

- *What might make you hesitate to share the gospel?*
  - *Comfort?*
  - *Security?*
  - *Significance?*
  - *Pain?*

- *How does the gospel that Paul describes here address your hesitations/concerns?*

HANDS:

In verses 7-13, Paul talks about the role of the church, encouraging them to be bold, confident, and persistent to make the manifold wisdom of God—the gospel—known to the world.

- *How can you and your community embrace this calling and encouragement?*

- *How can you be bold in making the grace of God known?*

- *How can the message of Ephesians be for your friends as well as for you?*

PRAY

Spend time praying for each other as you reflect on this passage and your own lives. Pray to be empowered by the Spirit as you walk in obedience.

WEEK 6

A Church with High Expectations

WEEK 6

Ephesians 3:14-21

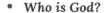

PERSONAL REFLECTION: FOUR QUESTIONS

Spend time reading this passage and reflecting on these questions in order. Think through all the explicit and implied statements about who God is, then what He has done, who we are, and how we should live. As you answer these questions, you can even connect them to each other. For example: If that's what God has done, who does that make me? And how do I live in light of that truth?

- **Who is God?**

- **What has He done?**

- **Who are we?**

- **How do we live?**

INTRODUCTION

With this prayer, Paul wraps up one large section on what God has done for us in the gospel and who the church is. Now, Paul turns his attention to encouraging and urging the church to be and live in accordance with their calling. Before he does that, he prays for us to know God's love.

This is quite the prayer. Quite the sentiment. The sort of thing that you put on coffee cups, that your grandmother puts on a pillow, and that you post on your bathroom mirror. It's poetic.

Often we can read the Bible, and in this case this rich letter to the Ephesians, and say, "Yeah, neat...'Know the surpassing love of Jesus,' that's great, but when will I get better friends, go on good vacations, or live 'the good life'?" Or we could think, "That's a cool prayer, for God to dwell richly within me, but when is my boss going to get off my back?" We might even be in moments of great pain in our lives and read this passage and jolt, "Sure, I could be filled with the fullness of God, but when will God heal me?" However, this is the prayer and anthem of the Church: knowing God is the greatest reward.

This prayer is *the* prayer. This is the vision of every church at all times. It's the vision of Christ for His Church that you—and every other believer—would be strengthened, empowered, and filled with the fullness of Christ. This is the main thing happening in your life. This is the main thing happening in my life. This is what God is doing. This prayer is about Revival. Renewal. Resurrection.

Jonathan Edwards said this about revival: "The true signs of revival in an individual, city, or church are when people are changed at the heart level." [2]

Honestly, this is what I see God doing in the midst of churches all over the world. Let's not get distracted. God is changing our hearts and making us more like him. Replacing selfishness with patience. Ego with love. Anxiety with peace. Lust with freedom. Loneliness with God's presence. Let's not lower our expectations for what God might do, but raise them.

Who wants to know the surpassing greatness of God's love? Who wants to know the fullness of God within them? Who wants to live in the power that raised Jesus from the dead? To see doubt moved to confidence? And even after all of those things, to walk away knowing that God could do far more than even that!

[2]In his essay to defend the Great Awakening, "Distinguishing Marks of Work of the Spirit of God."

READ EPHESIANS 3:14-21 OUT LOUD.

HEAD:

Discuss this passage together.

- *How does this prayer remind you of the character and motives of God already described in Ephesians?*

- *How does this prayer remind you of the gospel and fruit of the gospel from the previous passages in Ephesians?*

- *How does Paul pray, in light of the truth of the gospel, for extraordinary things for the church?*

- *How would you put this passage in your own words?*

PAUL'S PRAYERS ARE DIFFERENT

This prayer is so different than many of our typical prayers. We might tend to pray prayers that focus solely on our current situation. This is when we are simply asking God to change our circumstances and make our lives easier. There is a time for this kind of prayer, and we see examples of it throughout the Psalms. We'll call that circumstantial prayer. Often circumstantial prayer focuses on the temporal.

There is another kind of prayer that focuses on God changing us rather than Him changing our situation. This is how Paul prays. These are prayers related to people's character...prayers where we are asking God to make us and those in the Church "complete in Christ." Asking God to use our circumstances and challenges to grow us, to draw us closer to Him. We'll call that discipleship-focused prayer.

Discipleship-focused prayer often gets at the eternal prerogatives of God.

Paul writes in Colossians 1:28, "We proclaim Him, admonishing every man and teaching every man with all wisdom, so that we may present every man complete in Christ." We must, therefore, pray prayers that are aimed at this ultimate end. Otherwise our community is in danger of degenerating into, "God, would you please continue to make us more and more comfortable in every situation in our lives?" This is contrary to much of what we see in God's method of sanctification through the Scriptures and says much about our pursuit of comfort as an ultimate end. Do we share Paul's focus in striving to see everyone in this community presented complete in Christ? How will prayer factor into each person's development?

HEART:

Paul's prayer for the church not only teaches us about God and our expectations for life with God, it also teaches us that we need the power of God to even understand and comprehend the love of God.

- *Based on your discussion above, which truths are the easiest for you to believe?*

- *Which truths are the hardest to believe?*

- *Where do you need the Spirit's power to understand God's love?*

HANDS:

Spend time thinking through the implications of the first three chapters of Ephesians for your life.

- *If all of this is true, how should we live?*

- *If all of this is true, what will we do?*

PRAY

Spend time praying for each other as you reflect on this passage and your own lives. Pray to be empowered by the Spirit as you walk in obedience.

WEEK 7

A Church Transformed

WEEK 7

Ephesians 4:1-16

PERSONAL REFLECTION: FOUR QUESTIONS

Spend time reading this passage and reflecting on these questions in order. Think through all the explicit and implied statements about who God is, then what He has done, who we are, and how we should live. As you answer these questions, you can even connect them to each other. For example: If that's what God has done, who does that make me? And how do I live in light of that truth?

- *Who is God?*

- *What has He done?*

- *Who are we?*

- *How do we live?*

INTRODUCTION

Extremely Loud and Incredibly Close is the story of a family grappling with life in New York City after the death of their father, son, and husband in the attacks on the Twin Towers. A powerful moment comes with the image of the grandfather, who had survived incredible suffering during the Holocaust. He was a survivor and made it all the way to New York City only to abandon his wife and his son. He then spent his life living in an apartment across the street from his family, watching their lives but not engaged in them even after his son's horrible death on 9/11. In the end, he confesses this to his grandson, "Sometimes I can hear my bones straining under the weight of all the lives I'm not living."

We make the Christian life a set of virtues to follow, a list of rules to obey, a structure to dedicate ourselves to, a "state of being" we're just trying to hold together, a family tradition we're trying to keep. Or perhaps we consider it an add-on to the rest of our lives—church is not something we are, it's an organization we belong to.

When I observe what accounts for the Christian life today, I fear this could be our refrain: "Sometimes we hear our bones straining under the weight of all the lives we're not living."

Here Paul says it's more: a transformed life.

Paul shifts his letter ever so slightly to talk about how the mystery of the gospel transforms everything in our lives. This chapter contains some of the most powerful language of encouragement to live in light of the grace God has given us.

Paul describes something we struggle to fathom. We struggle to imagine a resurrection life. A life empowered by the same Spirit that conquered death. Paul tells us to have the courage to embrace a life that's far more reaching than knowing information and following disciplines. The power of the resurrection of Jesus is coursing through our hearts, minds, and life! You've been given not just a new round of living, but the abundant presence of Jesus in every facet of your existence. This is the life we've been given to live.

READ EPHESIANS 4:1-16 OUT LOUD.

HEAD:

Discuss this passage together.

- **What does this passage tell us about the Christian life? What is that life all about? Why do we live it?**

- **What does this passage tell us about Christian community?**

- **What is the goal of Christian community? What is your role in it?**

- **How would you put this passage in your own words?**

PARAKALEO

The word *parakaleo* means to encourage, to exhort, or very literally to call out in the most positive way. It's the word Jesus uses to describe the role of the Holy Spirit as a helper to empower us to live life.

Before this verse, Paul has been using language that can most simply be described as proclamation. He's been proclaiming the work of God in Jesus in the most eloquent and moving of terms. He's been declaring the excellence of this whole mystery of God's infinite love put directly on our souls. This is important language in the life of a church.

Later in Ephesians, Paul will use didactic language: teaching, instructing, sharing of wisdom: "Here's practically how to live and why. Here are the 'rules of life.' The imperatives. You must do _____."

What Paul is doing in Ephesians 4:1-16 is something that we miss all the time in the life of the ruckus of Christian community we call church. He is urging us to walk worthy of our calling. He's challenging us to live the life we've been given. It's the language of coming alongside a friend and saying: "Let us go on the journey of a lifetime. Let us go on the path of abundant joy. Let us live the full, abundant lives we were made for"....or as Paul writes: "I urge you, therefore, walk in a manner worthy of the calling to which you've been called."

HEART:

Often the Bible lands on us as truths to believe or rules to obey. Here, Paul is very clearly saying, there's a life to be lived in community and under the hope of Jesus. Where every part of life is filled with the singular love of God to us and in us.

- *How do you respond to that?*

- *What does that hit in your emotions? What distance is there between what you read and what you believe?*

- *Paul also describes the maturing of the body so we aren't tossed to and fro...what parts of your life feel chaotic?*

- *What messages do you believe that lead to emptiness?*

- *How would you put this passage in your own words?*

HANDS:

Here Paul is calling, urging, and encouraging us to walk worthy of the gospel.

- *How often are you encouraged to be who you were made to be?*

- *How regularly do you find yourself encouraging others?*

- *What does it mean for you to be called to abundant life? What does that feel like?*

- *What if we regularly spoke the truth in love to one another like that? What kind of community would we be if we urged one another?*

- *How can we encourage one another to walk worthy of the gospel this week? Be specific. If time allows, give space and opportunity for each person to name a specific area where they need the community to give encouragement or reminders to walk worthy of the gospel this week.*

PRAY

Spend time praying for each other as you reflect on this passage and your own lives. Pray to be empowered by the Spirit as you walk in obedience.

WEEK 8

A Messy Church

WEEK 8

Ephesians 4:17-32

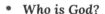

PERSONAL REFLECTION: FOUR QUESTIONS

Spend time reading this passage and reflecting on these questions in order. Think through all the explicit and implied statements about who God is, then what He has done, who we are, and how we should live. As you answer these questions, you can even connect them to each other. For example: If that's what God has done, who does that make me? And how do I live in light of that truth?

- **Who is God?**

- **What has He done?**

- **Who are we?**

- **How do we live?**

INTRODUCTION

To be honest, Ephesians 4:17 feels like a speed bump in this letter. It's jarring, it's shocking. It's like when you're driving on a gorgeous day with the windows down and the sun shining and life feels as it's supposed to be. Then you hit a pothole, and your car is now unaligned, and your phone falls off the phone holder on your dashboard, and your coffee goes flying, and you're left wondering, what happened to my good day? That's what Ephesians 4:17 feels like. At first glance.

Is Paul really calling people who aren't Christians dumb? Dense? Ignorant, impure, sex-demons?

Everything in this letter had been so powerful, so encouraging, as if it has some authority that transcends life, time, and culture. The truth of God's love, mercy, and resurrection wooed us into worship the last seven weeks. His urging to walk worthy was a paragraph of motivational writing unlike anything we find today. Then, there's this: "Do not walk like those people... with their futile minds." What's going on here? Why did Paul go so negative?

In reality, he's talking about us. He warns us to remember the truths of Jesus and constantly remind one another to pursue a perpetual renewal of our lives in the gospel—to refuse to return to the slavery of sin and the tyranny of a life with ourselves as god. He's encouraging us: don't go back into lies, but speak the gospel to one another and live it.

READ EPHESIANS 4:17-32 OUT LOUD.

HEAD:

Discuss this passage together.

- **What is Paul telling us to do and not do? Why?**

- **Why does God care about our lives?**

- **Who are we supposed to be?**

- **Who is God in the midst of our obedience and rebellion? Our remembering and our neglecting? (vs. 32)**

- **How would you put this passage in your own words?**

THE MESS IS ABOUT US

This passage is written to a people Paul assumed were a mess. He assumed the church of Ephesus had thieves in it (28). Alongside the thieves, he assumed were people prone to spouts of anger—both passive and aggressive. He also imagines the church is filled with foul-mouthed saints. Here's the beauty of these passages of Scripture that call Christians to be made new: they describe the church as messy redeemed sinners. It's as if all the people Jesus ate with—the prostitutes, thieves, tax collectors, and ragamuffins—found themselves in the church. I wonder, can we assume the same thing in our churches and communities? That we're all coming into this glorious family out of the mess?

When the church is tidy, or at least when the church is designed to look tidy, we don't see the mess, just the rugs with mounting dust tucked below them. If you embrace the gospel Paul has described in the opening chapters of this letter, and if you pray the prayers Paul has prayed in this letter, you'll discover an abundance of life in the power of the gospel to raise every sinner to life. You'll also find a boldness to declare your old life and the sins that still entangle you. And if you do that, you'll soon learn you're surrounded by saints who need to hear the same appeal: "Put off the old self and walk in the truth of Jesus."

HEART:

Sinclair Ferguson wrote in his book, *The Whole of Christ*: "The psychology of the old life can take much longer to shift than its theology." While our minds can repent and shift, the inner works of our attitudes, desires, and emotions often lag behind. Paul understood this. Throughout his letters, he urges believers to continually put off the old self.

In verses 25-32, Paul describes in more detail what taking off the old self and putting on the new self looks like as we grow into the likeness of Christ and live holy and righteous lives. He has several pairings. These outward actions readily overflow from our inward lives; they reflect what we believe. They demonstrate how we feel and believe and are truly our gut responses in life's circumstances. Which of these pairings stands out in your own life this past month? What does it tell you about what you believe (vs. 17-24)?

- *Falsehood vs. Speaking Truth to Neighbors*
- *Just Anger vs. Judgemental Anger*
- *Stealing for Yourself vs. Labor for Others*
- *Corrupt Talk vs. Building Each Other Up*
- *Malice & Wrath vs. Kindness & Tenderheartedness*
- *Bitterness vs. Forgiveness*

What are the effects on those around you when you live in the new self versus the old self? What does that feel like? What helps you pursue Christ in all of life?

HANDS:

- *What would it look like to pursue remembering Jesus in our everyday life?*

- *How will we pursue putting off our old selves and putting on our new selves in the power of the Holy Spirit?*

- *What difference would it make on the city around us if we lived our new identity?*

PRAY

Spend time praying for each other as you reflect on this passage and your own lives. Pray to be empowered by the Spirit as you walk in obedience.

WEEK 9

A CHURCH LIVING THE TRUTH

WEEK 9

Ephesians 5:1-21

PERSONAL REFLECTION: FOUR QUESTIONS

Spend time reading this passage and reflecting on these questions in order. Think through all the explicit and implied statements about who God is, then what He has done, who we are, and how we should live. As you answer these questions, you can even connect them to each other. For example: If that's what God has done, who does that make me? And how do I live in light of that truth?

- **Who is God?**

- **What has He done?**

- **Who are we?**

- **How do we live?**

INTRODUCTION

"Your actions speak louder than words."

"What you do reveals what you believe."

"Listen and obey."

"Walk in the way of love as Christ loved us and gave Himself up for us."

This is a paradigm shift. In chapter 5, Paul turns up the imperatives. He gives us commands and instructions to follow in each verse as he makes a case for the way of love, a life lived connecting the dots between what God has done, who we are, and how we get to live. He sums it all up in the beginning of the chapter: be imitators of Christ and walk in love.

We often idealize people in our professions who have gone where we want to be. We dress like them, plan our lives like them, and map our careers after them. Paul says here: pattern your entire life after the self-giving, powerful love of Jesus.

Over the next nineteen verses, he articulates very clearly what that means. What would a life of love look like? Some of it might surprise you, or at least surprise our cultural moment. There's a call to a robust sexual ethic, an ethic of language, an ethic to expose darkness (even the things hard to talk about), and a call to a meaningful spiritual life in community. But these aren't suggestions from an old man in prison. These are commands. Anyone who is in Christ is commanded by the authority of the Word of God to walk in love. Again, this is a radical paradigm shift.

READ EPHESIANS 5:1-21 OUT LOUD.

HEAD:

Discuss this passage together.

- **What does this passage tell us about Jesus and what He has done?**

- **Who does this passage say we are?**

- **How are we called to live and obey? It may be helpful to make a list.**

- **Why are we called to live this way?**

- **How would you put this passage in your own words?**

BEING BEFORE DOING— HOW WE LIVE FLOWS FROM WHO WE ARE

The type of language Paul uses and the way he writes this letter is intentionally instructive and theologically purposeful.

The first half of the letter is completely indicative. Meaning Paul outlines truths, facts, and writes authoritative statements on who God is, what He has done, and who we are. Paul says: This is the truth about God. This is the gospel of what God has done. Then, he says this is your identity: adopted children of God, His masterpiece, His people.

All of this comes before Paul writes any imperatives or commands. Identity comes first because who we are—and who we think we are—defines how we live. Jackie Hill Perry describes this truth well in her book, *Gay Girl, Good God*:

> Identity is a big deal. It, like a language we carry on our faces, says a lot of what we believe about God, ourselves, and others. Unable to help itself, it will determine the 'How' that governs our steps. The way we move about the world can always be traced back to the question, 'Who am I today?'
> **And 'What is God always?'**

In this passage, Paul connects the dots from who we are to how we live. The commands of the Scriptures are directly correlated to who we are.

However, we often flip the order. We think how we behave defines who we are. If we obey God, He will love us. If we perform, we can be included. If we're good enough, we can belong. This is legalism.

Or some of us go the other way. We think that since God loves us and gives us a new identity, it doesn't matter how we live. This is apathy, not just to our lives, but to the gospel itself. If how we live doesn't matter, why did Jesus die?

Paul carefully outlines in the book of Ephesians the reality of the gospel as good news about who God is, what He has done, who we are becoming because of it, and how we live because of who we are. In this passage, Paul answers the question: If we're infinitely loved and if we are God's people, how should we live? How do we live as the beloved children of light?

HEART:

In this passage, Paul calls out apathy, or "sleeping." He calls us to wake up! Apathy is one of the great indicators of something disconnected between our heads and our hearts.

- *Have you been in a season of apathy? Are you in that season now?*

- *What does apathy expose about what you believe?*

- *What is the good news of Jesus even in our apathy?*

HANDS:

These commands are not random; they're purposefully for our good and the good of those around us. Furthermore, they say something about Jesus to the world around us.

- *What would the impact of living a life completely submitted to Jesus look like?*

- *How would that affect those around you?*

- *What would change in our city if it saw a community living this way?*

- *How is the Spirit stirring your heart in response to our conversation and reading? Is there an area of your life where He's asking you to take a step of obedience?*

PRAY

Spend time praying for each other as you reflect on this passage and your own lives. Pray to be empowered by the Spirit as you walk in obedience.

WEEK 10

A Whole New Way of Relating

WEEK 10

Ephesians 5:15-6:9

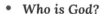 PERSONAL REFLECTION: FOUR QUESTIONS

Spend time reading this passage and reflecting on these questions in order. Think through all the explicit and implied statements about who God is, then what He has done, who we are, and how we should live. As you answer these questions, you can even connect them to each other. For example: If that's what God has done, who does that make me? And how do I live in light of that truth?

- **Who is God?**

- **What has He done?**

- **Who are we?**

- **How do we live?**

INTRODUCTION

Genesis 3 is about the breaking of the world through sin, death, and evil. They are a tidal wave that overtakes every corner of the cosmos and every facet of every human relationship. They produce anxiety, stress, abuse, pain, and ultimately the destruction of human life. Human relationships from that first moment under the tree with Adam and Eve until you and me are the tip of the spear of sin's damages. The curse of sin nestles itself into the center of all marriages, all families, all workplaces, and all teams.

Ephesians is about a world reshaped by the power of resurrection and a people born out of the unending grace of Jesus. This is good news about a new reality that Paul calls a masterpiece. What if every human relationship was made alive in Christ too? What if the curse of sin not only reconciled us to God, but made us reconcilers to one another? What if Jesus raised every broken relationship back to life?

What would that look like? In Christ, Paul is saying that starts today! The Holy Spirit of God in His Church creates a society of saints...saints who are marked by a way of love in all their relationships.

When I read this passage, I greet it with excitement: This is what happens in every relationship when love comes to church and dwells richly and deeply within us. Relationships in complete unity. Relationships without the curse or stain of sin.

READ EPHESIANS 5:15-6:9 OUT LOUD.

HEAD:

Discuss this passage together.

- *While it can be hard with a passage like this, first discuss who you see Jesus to be in this passage. What do you learn about His character, His actions, His desires?*

- *How does the Church submit to Christ?*

- *How do our relationships tell the story of the gospel and reflect the character of Jesus?*

- *How are we called to live in these relationships? What does obedience look like?*

- *How would you put this passage in your own words?*

REVERENCE TO CHRIST AND SUBMISSION

Paul writes, "Submit one to another out of reverence for Christ." This word *submission* means to yield to and to consider with great weight. A clear and constant distinction in the life of all followers is submission. In fact, many of the commands can easily be summed up as submission. Consider, with great weight, your neighbor, their life, their passions, their needs, their desires. Or, yield to one another. Put your life below and behind the needs of those in your community. To be a saint is to be submitted: to Christ, to one another, to your neighbor.

Here, Paul takes it further. He says there's a direct correlation to how much time we spend listening to and watching Jesus and how we treat one another. How we view Jesus (His authority, His love for us, His glory) directly overflows into how we live like Jesus together in all horizontal relationships. Are you submitted to Jesus? That's the headline news of this passage. The subtitle is: Are you submitted to one another? In your marriage? In your family? In your work?

HEART:

This passage of Ephesians is the cause of many contentious conversations. It's often been abused and been used to abuse others. However, it's a glorious text that does two things: It challenges every heart in every role of life, and it speaks hope into every wound in relationships.

- *How have you disrespected, disregarded, provoked, people-pleased, threatened, or been selfish towards others?*

- *How have you felt disrespected, disregarded, provoked, dishonored, ignored, or threatened by others?*

- *How does the gospel of Jesus bring life to those sins and wounds?*

- *What does a life of repentance look like?*

HANDS:

Paul is describing a wonderfully submitted and powerful collection of saints.

- *How would your neighborhood be transformed if it had a regular encounter with a community that "submitted one to another out of reverence to Jesus?"*

- *What would that submission look like?*

- *What is an area of your life where you sense the Spirit asking you to submit to Jesus as you submit to others in your life? What are the hardest areas of life to submit to Jesus?*

PRAY

Spend time praying for each other as you reflect on this passage and your own lives. Pray to be empowered by the Spirit as you walk in obedience.

WEEK 11

A Church at War

WEEK 11

Ephesians 6:10-23

PERSONAL REFLECTION: FOUR QUESTIONS

Spend time reading this passage and reflecting on these questions in order. Think through all the explicit and implied statements about who God is, then what He has done, who we are, and how we should live. As you answer these questions, you can even connect them to each other. For example: If that's what God has done, who does that make me? And how do I live in light of that truth?

- **Who is God?**

- **What has He done?**

- **Who are we?**

- **How do we live?**

INTRODUCTION

I believe if you gave me the book of Ephesians and the entire *Band of Brothers* series, I would be good for a lifetime of learning and growth! They're both filled with so much truth, wisdom, and challenge. *Band of Brothers* tells the story of a single group of men who go from basic training to the end of World War II as paratroopers. These ordinary men went on to fight in the most significant battles in France, Belgium, Holland, and Germany. Every mission they had was to get loaded up with all the supplies they would need and then jump out of a plane thousands of feet above and behind enemy lines. From the moment they left the plane, they were surrounded. The battle didn't come to them; they jumped into it.

On the evening before D-Day, their first mission, their commanders walk through the airfield explaining the mission, summarizing their goals, and making sure each member was well equipped, confident, and ready. I believe that's exactly what Paul is doing at the closing of this letter to the Ephesians. He's reminding the church we have a mission, it's dangerous, but we have everything we need!

There is a realm in the unseen that is motivated, personal, evil, and set on the destruction of the joy of God's Church and the dulling of the Church's mission. There is more than what we see and know. It's not sociological, psychological, or physical, but spiritual. There's a spiritual reality that's both powerful and anti-gospel.

Paul ends Ephesians with an appeal to embrace this battle. But more deeply, to remember the power of God to raise us from the dead and that the victory of Jesus is cosmic in nature, comprehensive in scope, and catastrophic to all evil. Jesus has won and given that victory to the Church as our inheritance. This isn't a passage about defense from the world, but about a confident and gracious offensive into the world, knowing we're armed with the power to raise souls from the dead.

READ EPHESIANS 6:10-23 OUT LOUD.

HEAD:

Discuss this passage together.

- Where does our strength come from? Where do you see that in the rest of Ephesians?

- What are we battling against and what victory has been won (looking at earlier passages)?

- Where do you see the "armor" in the previous passages?

- How would you put this passage in your own words?

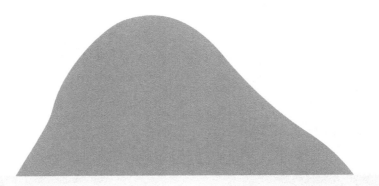

TWO EXTREMES

Often with spiritual warfare, there are two extremes. On one extreme, many say, "There's no such thing as evil spiritual forces," and on the other, people say, "The devil is behind everything!" These two extremes get played out in dangerous ways. Ignoring or refusing to see the power of darkness in our world, our communities, and our personal lives limits our readiness. On the other hand, when the devil is the reason for every difficult circumstance, we fail to see the sovereign grace of God even in suffering.

The reality is there is a real personal presence of evil. It's creepy, and it's ordinary. It isn't random or irregular—it's constant, and it's strategic. The evil spiritual forces come to us not creating havoc in our agendas, but havoc with our beliefs, our faith, and our zeal in following Jesus into the grand mission of God. C.S. Lewis wrote: "The enemy will not see you vanish into God's company without an effort to reclaim you." That's exactly what is going on.

HEART:

Here's what the enemy does amidst all the circumstances of life: He lies. The devil lies to reclaim you, neutralize you, and steal your life. These lies are the common weapons and schemes of the devil:

1. *You are above this situation.*
2. *You are below this situation.*
3. *If you were better, it would be easier.*
4. *If it isn't happening now, it never will.*
5. *You are alone.*

The spiritual forces of evil will not stop until you're bathed in lies—until you're so busy, distracted by comfort, or disillusioned by circumstances you will not utter a word of worship to God nor a word of hope to those around you.

- *Which of these lies do you hear the most?*

- *How do these lies keep us from joy, Jesus, and the mission of God?*

- *What power does God have over these lies?*

- *If time allows, walk through each of the lies above and name the specific truths of God that combat them. Cite specific passages in Scripture for each.*

HANDS:

Verses 18-20 are the key to this passage. They describe the purpose of this battle and the battlefield itself. They're about the proclamation of the greatest hope with extraordinary boldness. Timothy Chester describes and summarizes this reality in his book *The Message of Prayer*:

> Spiritual warfare is not about naming territorial spirits, claiming the ground, or binding demons. It is all about the gospel. It is to live a gospel life, to preserve gospel unity and to proclaim gospel truth. It is to do this in the face of a hostile world, a deceptive enemy, and our sinful natures. And it is to pray to a *sovereign God for gospel opportunities*. Advance comes through godliness, unity, proclamation and prayer.

- **What kind of life would require ongoing prayer for endurance?**

- **What would happen if we boldly proclaimed the mystery of the gospel?**

- **How can we live as ambassadors in chains?**

- **How is the Spirit calling you to respond? How is He stirring in you in light of this conversation?**

PRAY

Spend time praying for each other as you reflect on this passage and your own lives. Pray to be empowered by the Spirit as you walk in obedience.

WEEK 12

Being the Church

WEEK 12

Now, let's pause and consider, how will we move forward transformed by the Word? How will our community live out these truths?

HEAD:

Read the entire book of Ephesians out loud together. You can take turns reading each paragraph. As you read, remember what you learned and remember your discussions.

Answer the following questions. Make sure you have someone writing down the answers as a "scribe" of sorts.

- *What have we learned about who God is?*

- *What have we learned about what God has done, is doing, and will do?*

- *What have we learned about who we are in Christ?*

- *What have we learned about the Church?*

- *What have we learned about how we should live?*

HEART:

Answer the following questions and read your answers out loud. Spend time reflecting on the gaps between what you've learned and what you believe.

- *How have our beliefs changed?*

- *What areas of life need healing?*

- *What areas of life need repentance?*

- *What are we struggling to believe?*

HANDS:

Now comes the challenge: how will your community be different? How will you plan, organize, and commit to a new way of being based on the Scriptures? The following questions are intended to help frame that conversation and lead to specific commitments.

- *How will we change as a community to live out the realities of the gospel and our identity?*

- *How will you speak the gospel to one another?*

- *What needs to change in our community?*

- *What needs to be declared to those outside our community?*

- *How will we commit to being the Church in the upcoming months?*

PRAYER AND WORSHIP:

For this final week, spend time in prayer and worship, thanking God for who He is, what He has done, and who He has declared we are because of Jesus, and asking Him to help us walk worthy of His call and obedient to His Spirit.

Suggestion: This could also be a great moment to take communion together as you acknowledge your community's need for Jesus and praise Him for giving Himself for you and calling you into His Church and mission. How can you do this? Jeff Vanderstelt shares how he structures communion in community to focus on the gospel in this short video (*http://bit.ly/ MCcommunion*).

FINAL WORD

Ephesians is our letter. This is our moment of the story. This is who we are. We are the Church, created by the gospel of Jesus for the sake of the gospel of Jesus. He's given us every spiritual blessing and all power to embody the mission He's given us. Let's take this letter not merely as information to add into our mental filing cabinet, but as the words of God that transform us and our cities, towns, and villages. Whatever you've written on the final week, expand your imagination for what God might do in you and through you. He can do more than you could ever imagine because He already has when He raised you from the dead.

-PAUL, EPHESIANS 3:20-21

Now to him who is able to do far more abundantly than all that we ask or think, according to the power at work within us, to him be glory in the church and in Christ Jesus throughout all generations, forever and ever. Amen.

GLOSSARY

Missional Community–A missional community is a group of people learning to follow Jesus together in a way that renews our city. They aren't fancy. In fact, they can be pretty messy communities of everyday citizens devoted to Jesus, to one another, and to their neighbors.

The Gospel–"Gospel" simply means "good news" and is the pronouncement concerning the person and work of Jesus Christ. It is all about Jesus: He is God and became a man, lived the most abundant life with God and others without sin. Jesus died the death we should have died, as our substitute. Jesus rose from the dead, conquering sin and its effects.

The Power of the Gospel–The gospel is the power of God to save (Romans 1:9). Through Jesus's death and resurrection we have been saved from the penalty of sin (justification), we are being saved from the power of sin (sanctification), and we will be saved from the presence of sin. This means the same power that saved us from the penalty of sin also helps us obey God now. (Ephesians 2:8-9; Colossians 1:27-29; 2:6-7)

The Purpose of the Gospel–The good news is also that God sent His Son to redeem the world from the effects of sin and create a new humanity. Eventually, the whole world will be renewed to the way God originally created it. Rebellion, death, decay, injustice, and suffering will all be removed. When everything is restored, God will be seen by all for who He truly is–He will be glorified. (Ephesians 2:10,14-22; 2 Corinthians 5:15-21; Revelation 21)

The Story of God—The Bible is not just a list of rules to obey, stories to be inspired by, or morals to live your life by. Sure, the Bible contains rules, stories, and morality, but it is so much more than just these things. It is the true story of the world. It is a divine drama. It is a dramatic six-act play: Creation, Rebellion, Promise, Redemption, The Church, Restoration.

Identity—We aren't defined by what we do. We are defined by what God has done in the person and work of Jesus Christ. What we do is based upon and motivated by who God is, what God has done, and who God has made us to be. The New Testament doesn't define the Church by activities, buildings, or programs. Instead, the Church is defined by God—the Father, Son, and Holy Spirit. In the gospel, we receive a new identity.

SATURATE MEMBERSHIP

We receive the most requests for resources and connection. The Saturate Membership is designed to meet both needs. Membership to Saturate's resource site offers both individual and group access to hundreds of video, print, and digital resources designed to help you and your church implement a gospel-centered disciple-making culture.

The Saturate online community connects disciple-making practitioners all over the world to interact on a variety of topics and offer shared experience and encouragement.

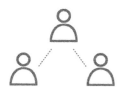

Get started today and get your first month free with this coupon code: FIRSTMONTH

Visit **www.saturatetheworld.com/membership** to sign up and to get more information.

Made in the USA
Columbia, SC
31 August 2019